ideals® CHRISTMAS

More Than 50 Years of Celebrating Life's Most Treasured Moments

Vol. 58, No. 6

May the Christmas miracle of love, hope, peace, and joy blossom in your heart.
—*Author Unknown*

Featured Photograph
6

Country Chronicle
10

Traveler's Diary
16

For the Children
20

Bits and Pieces
22

Through My
Window
32

The Nativity
38

Devotions from
the Heart
48

Remember When
54

Readers' Reflections
58

A Slice of Life
60

Legendary Americans
64

Handmade Heirloom
66

Ideals' Family Recipes
72

From My
Garden Journal
76

Collector's Corner
78

Readers' Forum
86

IDEALS—Vol. 58, No. 6 November MMI IDEALS (ISSN 0019-137X, USPS 256-240)
is published six times a year: January, March, May, July, September, and November by
IDEALS PUBLICATIONS, a division of Guideposts
39 Seminary Hill Road, Carmel, NY 10512.
Copyright © MMI by IDEALS PUBLICATIONS, a division of Guideposts.
All rights reserved. The cover and entire contents of IDEALS are fully protected by copyright
and must not be reproduced in any manner whatsoever.
Title IDEALS registered U.S. Patent Office. Printed and bound in USA by Quebecor Printing.

Printed on Weyerhaeuser Husky. The paper used in this publication meets the minimum requirements of
American National Standard for Information Sciences—
Permanence of Paper for Printed Library Materials, ANSI Z39.48-1984.

Periodicals postage paid at Carmel, New York, and additional mailing offices.
POSTMASTER: Send address changes to Ideals, 39 Seminary Hill Road, Carmel, NY 10512.
For subscription or customer service questions, contact Ideals Publications,
a division of Guideposts, 39 Seminary Hill Road, Carmel, NY 10512. Fax 845-228-2115.

Reader Preference Service: We occasionally make our mailing lists available to
other companies whose products or services might interest you.
If you prefer not to be included, please write to Ideals Customer Service.

ISBN 0-8249-1170-9 GST 893989236

Visit *Ideals*'s website at www.idealspublications.com

Cover Photo: Festive Lampposts. Photo by Daniel Dempster.
Artwork this page: Ginger. Stacy Venturi Pickett, Artist.
Inside Front Cover: CHRISTMAS ROSES. *William Jabez Muckley, Artist. Image from Fine Art Photographic Library Ltd./Julian Simon Gallery.*
Inside Back Cover: A GLOWING CHRISTMAS HEARTH. *Artist Unknown. Image from Fine Art Photographic Library Ltd.*

Wondrous Love

Emily May Young

Now holy Christmastime is here once more.
We linger in that story centuries old.
The glistening snow, the wreath-trimmed door
Present a picture of the story told
In scenes surpassing any festival.
And now the joyous carol singers come;
Their lyric voices sweetly mystical
Shall carry messages to Christendom.

And gently on the cold December air
The haunting loveliness of "Silent Night"
Renews the picture, living, still as fair
As when the Child first slept in candlelight.
We feel good will on earth and toward mankind,
A wondrous love to heal the troubled mind.

Aspen trees catch the light in Wyoming's Bridger-Teton National Forest. Photo by Fred Pflughoft/Gnass Photo Images.
INSET: A wreath welcomes forest visitors. Photo by Nancy Matthews.

Christmas Snow

Jean Gier

A softly falling Christmas snow
Adorns the darkened woods below;
The regal pines that crown the hill
Conceal a stately stag and doe.

A rabbit flees the midnight chill
And scampers home beyond the rill
Through crystal vines, a nimble flight
To reach its burrow, warm and still.

A single star of silver light
Is twinkling from a distant height
Till woods, imbued with wintry white,
Sleep bejeweled on Christmas night.

Silver Silence

Ruth B. Field

So silently the crystal snowflakes fell
While all the winter birds forgot to sing.
And hushed was every listening tower bell;
Deep silence hovered like a silvery wing.
In wonder, each tree stood so very still;
The murmuring brook song faded quite away.
While velvet piled high on each windowsill
And falling white stars blurred the winter day,
Deep silence fell upon the countryside.
Small, muffled sounds came at last, when lo!
A star bloomed o'er the hill at eventide.
It seemed that angels sang across the snow.

*Left: Ponderosa pines, covered with ice, stand
statue-like in California's Northern Sierra
Nevada. Photo by Carr Clifton.
Overleaf: A snowy landscape surrounds
Virginia's Blackwater Falls. Photo by Carr Clifton.*

Winter Blessings

Mildred L. Jarrell

When winter winds with keenness blow
And twilight brings the falling snow,
Then lighted hearth fires flare and bloom,
Dispelling shadows round the room.

When family gathers for the night
To talk before the embers bright,
To join in games and lively song,
We know the warmth and love of home.

When all outdoors is wrapped in snow
And windows shine with candle glow,
We bask in blessings heaven sent
Before the fire and are content.

Neighbors

Rena Chandler

I look across my garden plot,
Now covered with its blanket white,
To where my neighbors' homes are set.
I see their glowing lamps alight
And hearth smoke rising happily
From rooftops, while the crystal snow
Is curling soft along the eaves
That wrap the gathered folk below.
I smile to know them near and feel
Companionship that warms my heart,
The night enfolding each and all,
The love of which we are a part.

A snowman greets neighbors in Westminster, Vermont.
Photo by Dick Dietrich/Dietrich Photography.

Country
CHRONICLE
Lansing Christman

CHRISTMAS WALK

My Christmas walk this year will be a walk through not only the snowy winter landscape, but through my memory as well. It will begin in the fields and meadows where hay and grain once grew. For a while I will follow the pasture creek and listen to the waters murmur under the ice as they wind their way among the rocks and stones and down the precipices. I will hear the calls of the chickadees from the creek-bank hemlocks and walk toward the old woods with its beech and oak and hemlock. I will cross the creek at the top of the thirty-foot waterfall to enter the new woods with its pine and cedar and spruce, the woods I helped plant as a boy and a man. I know these woods, the old and the new, and I am a part of them.

Following the top of the hill along the line fence, I will turn north again and down the hill to a flatland where timothy once grew. There I will climb over the stone wall into the pasture where cattle and horses grazed long ago. It's growing trees now, trees planted by nature. My journey will take me to a stony ledge where the witch-hazel grows, and I will stop by a pasture pine where I once had a play-house between two large outcroppings of rock. Nearby is the marsh where I first heard the courtship song of the woodcock seventy-five Aprils ago.

Then crossing the creek that separates the pasture from the dooryard, I'll climb the wall and once again be at the doorstep of the ancestral home where I was born more than ninety years ago. My meandering walk will take me through the snow from a home and landscape of today back to a home and place that will forever live in my heart and in my memories.

The author of three books, Lansing Christman has contributed to Ideals *for almost thirty years. Mr. Christman has also been published in several American, foreign, and braille anthologies. He lives in rural South Carolina.*

At a tree farm in Bethlehem, New Hampshire, tiny trees aspire to future holidays in the spotlight.
Photo by William H. Johnson.

A snowy path leads to home in SNOWSCAPE (AFTER DENT) *by artist Bert Litsch. Image from Superstock.*

DECEMBER

Gladys Taber

The first real snow comes usually the first week in December, a prelude to winter (which officially begins the twenty-first). A few feathers drift down, so casually that I wonder whether it is really snow or a bit of white ash from the incinerator. I check the sky and see they are definitely coming down. It won't amount to anything, says everyone at the market. But I notice we all stock up with extra supplies, in case it should amount to something!

There is an excitement about this first snow, and I've wondered why. I think it is because we face up to winter, after a lot of useless trying to put it off. Here it is, the challenge, as it has always been. I think if we suddenly had a bit of Florida now, we should be upset.

"Guess we're in for a hard one," says Joe.

"Yup, that's what the woolly bears say," comments George.

"Hope you all have plenty of wood," says Louis.

"Days are getting mighty short," remarks Steve.

"I made it thirteen above this morning," says Mr. Bennett.

Ski jumpers must have some of the same sensation as they poise at the top of the dangerous run. This is it, here we go! . . .

The first snow intoxicates the cockers and Holly. They reel around the yard, snapping at snowflakes. When they come in the house they are frosted with stars. The house will be damp from now on; so will the sofa covers, but I tell myself moisture is good for a house. The dogs are good humidifiers.

The big snow generally comes toward Christmas, although occasionally we have a green Christmas, which disappoints the children. I look for a big storm around Christmas and another over New Year's. This may be just an idea due to the years when the children came home from school for the holidays and it always seemed almost impossible to meet their trains or get to them at the end of vacation. When the snow is falling so thickly that one cannot see the front of the car, it can take an hour-and-a-half for the ten-minute trip to the nearest town with a railroad station. . . .

I do not enjoy being chilled to my bone marrow, and I often look at the dazzling pictures of the beaches at Hawaii after I take off three layers of woolens. I think a person would have a fine life in Hawaii or Florida or California or any place where there is no winter. Everyone has dreams, and I sometimes dream of never wearing wraps, of living in eternal summer. And always on a day of the worst sleet storm I have letters from friends who tell me the roses are blooming where they are and it is so hot they read what I write of winter so they can cool off.

A house would not seem as snug unless winter walked around outside.

At this point I feel silly putting on my boots and storm jacket just to go out to fill the bird feeders.

I can only conclude that those of us who are New Englanders do not transplant well. It wouldn't seem natural not to have the great storms of winter, the knife-sharp cold, the snow piling against the picket fence. A house would not seem as snug unless winter walked around outside. And there would never be the excitement of finally being able to get the car out and drive to the village. If you could hop in any minute and whisk away, there would be nothing special about being able to get two miles to the village.

And nothing can compare in any land in any climate with the way we feel when the snow melts, the brooks run free, and the peepers make their chilly sweet song in the swamp. Without winter, we should not have the special miracle of spring.

In December, we look toward spring, but on the way, we get a great deal of joy out of such things as a warm house, a good woodpile, and a world of silver outside. We feel triumph when we get the car motor to catch and a great satisfaction when we negotiate the snow-deep roads. We love winter parties when everyone turns up saying they had to dig out three times. It means they really did want to come!

I sometimes wonder whether New Englanders are just born peculiar, but then I look at the purity of snow and the pattern of dark branches against the sky, and I decide we are not queer at all. We just like four seasons a year.

The Yule log burns to ash and becomes a thing remembered. The Twelfth-night greens crackle on the hearth and then they too are gone. The Christmas tree ornaments are packed away and put in the attic. The old house settles with a sigh. It is time to put the thermostat down, get a storm jacket on, and step into boots.

The cockers and Holly are already at the door and rush out ahead of me. They all stop to munch snow and then roll in it. After that, they dash across the yard barking at nothing. I take a few steps feeling the snow crunch pleasantly. When the dogs quiet down, there is no sound at all. Stillmeadow is an island in the winter night, but I can see three lights up the hill across Jeremy Swamp Road.

The moon seems to stand still, and the stars are like daffodils in the meadows of the sky. If I breathe softly, I might hear the music of the spheres, or so it seems. I am in a moment out of time. I hold the universe in my hand and understand the meaning of all things.

And then I hear the neighbor's beagle baying in the old orchard and my dogs answer. I am in the familiar world again, in my valley, in winter. But I know the season moves on, the pulsing life of spring will spread a green veil over meadows and hills, the warm tide of summer will brim the hollows, and autumn will blaze against the sky.

As I go in to the fire, the words of faith come once more: "And on earth peace, good will toward men."

Child of the North

Norma West Linder

I was young in the snow;
Young in the sunbeam's darting dance,
Young in the moonlight's gentle glow.
I was immortal
In the snow.

I loved the chill of icicle air,
The taste of snowflakes on my tongue,
My mittened hands upon the sleigh,
The winds that forced my feet to run
Into today.

Now I no longer run,
But I often pause on a moon-bright night,
Gathering diamonds from fields of white
With hungry eyes.

Right: A family prepares for a sleigh ride in Burlington, Vermont. Photo by Bill Tucker/International Stock. Above: A child discovers the delights of snow. Photo by Tom and Michele Grimm/International Stock.

AURORA BOREALIS

ALASKA

Amy Johnson

I have had the privilege of living in some pretty interesting places in my lifetime. I was born in England and lived in Norway and Colorado as a youth. But when I moved with my family to Alaska as a young teen, I knew I had encountered a special place. Alaska, or the Last Frontier, as the state is nicknamed, boasts Mount McKinley, the tallest mountain in North America; and numerous species of wildlife, including moose, bear, and caribou. Its chilly night skies are also home to something quite mysterious. My most vivid memories of Alaska center around the aurora borealis—the sometimes eerie, always beautiful "northern lights" that dazzle the winter skies and, in my mind, truly represent the spirit of the Last Frontier.

Ancient Native Alaskans associated the lights with an unseen spiritual force. Before science was able to explain what caused the northern lights, Alaskan people such as the Athabaskans believed the aurora borealis represented the spirits of their ancestors who were watching over them. Although scientists now know that the northern lights are caused by charged particles from the sun which collide with Earth's magnetic field in its upper atmosphere, I could sense with each aurora sighting that the lights in some way represented the protection and care, not of my ancestors, but of the One who created both man and nature. The streaks of colored light I often saw in the northern skies were visible anywhere from forty to six hundred miles above the earth. At higher altitudes, they appeared bright red in color, whereas at lower altitudes they produced a yellowish-green hue. Both colors were equally magnificent and created in me a sense of awe and wonder at the handiwork of Him who put the mysterious lights in the northern sky.

I was continually amazed at the different ways in which the northern lights paraded across the night sky. Sometimes the lights appeared as bright patches of color, randomly dotting the sky; at other times the lights looked like a rainbow's arc; and in rare instances, they appeared as a curtain draping the sky from east to west. In addition to their constantly changing appearance, the lights also seemed to take on a personality of their own. Occasionally they were completely still and conveyed a deep sense of peacefulness as they softly lit up the sky. They could also flash rapidly across the horizon and disappear within seconds, almost as if they too felt the cold and were in no hurry to linger in it.

The aurora borealis are usually seen late at night, in the early hours just before daybreak. Perhaps that is why, in 1621, French scientist Pierre Gassendi named them after Aurora, the Roman goddess of the dawn. He then added the word *borealis* as a tribute to Boreas, the Roman god of the north wind. Despite the late hours at which the lights were visible and the chilly north winds I had to brave, I eagerly looked for the northern lights at every opportunity. On especially cold, clear nights when I knew there was a greater chance of the lights making their appearance, I would bundle up in my parka, take a blanket from the living room, and stand in my driveway to watch the sky. I was never disappointed in the scenes that appeared above me.

Once I saw the lights look like drapery across the sky. They were soft yellow and green in color, and their presence was breathtaking. The lights were perfectly calm and still as they illuminated the towering mountains nearby. I was so wrapped up in the scene before me that I completely forgot how

The aurora borealis fill the night sky over Alaska. Photo by Superstock.

cold it was. Although it was undoubtedly fifteen degrees below zero, I stood outside for about ten minutes, spellbound at the peaceful glow above me. Then the lights disappeared just as suddenly as they had appeared, and I went inside to warm up with a cup of hot chocolate and to reflect upon the beauty I had just witnessed.

Another time, shortly before Christmas, my family and I were visiting some friends when we were told by their ten-year-old son to "come outside, quickly!" We dashed to the front porch and immediately gazed heavenward, where we saw the lights dance merrily across the sky in brilliant greens flecked with pale red. High above the lights were hundreds of golden stars. With Christmas only a few weeks away, I was reminded of the light that had guided the wise men to the manger. It seemed as though God was reminding us of His love through those dazzling lights, just as He had reminded the wise men of His love by pointing them to the Christ Child. With these thoughts warming my heart, it was easy to stand in the chilly night air for several more minutes and revel in the spectacular colors swirling across the night sky.

My memories of the northern lights are ones I will treasure for many years, especially since I now live in Tennessee and can no longer enjoy those heavenly displays as I once did. To me, the northern lights not only represented the spirit of Alaska; they also communicated the power of God's handiwork and the brilliance of His creation. And even though I know that science can now explain many natural phenomena, including the lights in the northern skies, it is somehow reassuring to think that, just as God communicated to the wise men with a star long ago, He speaks to us today through His creation, which includes the magnificent northern lights.

OUR CHRISTMAS STAR

Shirley Bryan Wright

We have a star so tarnished
That its gold is dull and dark.
The brilliance of its tinsel
Long ago has lost its spark.

And yet we take it gently
From its tissue paper nest
To hang upon our Christmas tree—
A crown upon its crest.

For there were little faces
Who once gazed with widened eyes
And fancied that this shining star
Came straight down from the skies.

This star has seen our circle grow,
Has warmed each girl and boy;
It cast its benedictive light
On every grief and joy.

So hang it up another year,
This battered, age-old gem;
For memories will make it blaze
Like the star of Bethlehem.

For Christ is reborn in each heart
that follows the Christmas star.

—NICK KENNY

*The prize of the tree-trimming party waits its turn.
Photo by Garry Gay/International Stock.*

FOR THE CHILDREN

Bundles

John Farrar

A bundle is a funny thing.
It always sets me wondering:
For whether it is thin or **wide**
You never know just what's inside.

Especially in Christmas week
Temptation is so great to peek!
Now wouldn't it be much more fun
If shoppers carried things undone?

BITS & PIECES

My door is open wide tonight,
The hearth fire is aglow;
I seem to hear swift passing feet,
The Christ Child in the snow.
—*Author Unknown*

Again Christmas: abiding point of return . . .
All that is dear, that is lasting, renews its hold
on us: we are home again.
—*Elizabeth Bowen*

The chimneys of peace on the roofs of snow
Keep watch, and the world is still.
—*Esther M. Wood*

God bless the master of this house,
The mistress also,
And all the little children
That round the table go.
—*Author Unknown*

Let every doorstep have a song
Sounding the dark street along
In the week when Christmas comes.

—*Eleanor Farjeon*

Each house is swept the day before,
And windows stuck with evergreens;
The snow is besomed from the door,
And comfort crowns the cottage scenes.

—*John Clare*

It is Christmas in the mansion,
Yule-log fires and silken frocks.
It is Christmas in the cottage;
Mother's filling little socks.

—*Author Unknown*

Now not a window small or big
But wears a wreath or holly sprig.

—*Rachel Field*

Remembered Christmas

Julia Hurd Strong

It was Christmas Eve in the old homestead
With windows draped in the same rich red
That everyone present remembered well
From his first year under the Christmas spell.
The Christmas tree, pine-sweet and tall,
Had its sparse side pressed against the wall
And its spire branch topped by a homemade star
Snipped from tin by an ancestor
Long forgotten. The gifts were trapped
I*n all their* ...tly wrapped
...as so thin
...ecrets in.
...or opened wide
...drafts inside,
...to kiss those seen
...he months between
...e might believe
...Christmas Eve,
...s Eve before—
...hundred more—
...iving and dead,
...the old homestead.

...e at Christmas,
...d years.
...of the day,
...rs.

Alice Leedy Mason

...emember. Photo by Jessie Walker.

The Song and the Star

Grace V. Watkins

My father had the shining gift of song.
His voice was cello-beautiful and strong.
Oh, sometimes, listening to the choir where he
Gave humble, dedicated ministry,
I felt I stood with shepherds, hearing bright
Allegro anthems syllabled with light;
Then came with gladness to the manger place
And looked upon the Christ Child's holy face.

My mother had the gift of quietness.
How often her tranquility would bless
My weariness with peace! And in her eyes
It often seemed I saw the star arise
In silent majesty so calm and fair
My heart was filled with wonderment of prayer,
As though that star, more lovely than a gem,
Were leading me to the Child of Bethlehem.

What sweet, what priceless memories they are:
The golden-echoing song, the quiet star!

*Christmas is a golden chain that binds a
family in faith, hope, and love . . . drawing
each to the open hearth of togetherness.*

—Juanita Johnson

*A favorite Christmas carol echoes through holiday memories.
Photo by Nancy Matthews.*

Snowbound

Ralph Speer

It was worth being stranded for two days
To watch him on the sled.
All that spinning, sputtering, and shoveling
Disappeared like a poorly aimed snowball
When I put his joy on a rudder
And giggled him down the hill.
Then we warmed at the window,
Watching his puppy bark at a drift.

Picture That Cheers

Mary C. Ferris

The canvas is ready, the slope gleaming white,
Freshly covered with snowfall the previous night.
And now for the colors, the greens and the reds,
The bright little snowsuits of children with sleds.
In cap and mitt, brilliant as wool can be dyed,
They weave in and out and they tumble and slide.
Framed by my window, this picture still cheers
The grave, sedate hearts of grown-up years.

*A young sledder tries to urge his canine companion
onward in* Don't Stop Now *by artist D. R. Laird.
Image copyright © Mountain Rendezvous
Publishing Limited.*

Pageant at Christmas

Ruth Ebberts

We have come in on wind-swept winter night
To witness once again those scenes of old;
Here wise men kneel and children robed in white
Are caroling while shepherds watch the fold.
Here is the manger where the Christ Child lies,
With Mary wrapped in cloth of softest blue;
The light of heaven shines, and starry eyes
Behold the Babe. All that is good and true
Flows through the air while humble hearts rejoice.
A pageant, but we find our faith restored.
And lauding Him who granted right-of-choice,
We whisper with the children, "Praise the Lord."

By coming in to view a Christmas play,
We sense anew the joy of Christmas Day.

It's Christmas Everywhere

Patricia Ann Emme

The children sing so soft and low;
The church bells ring above the snow;
The holy star shines bright and clear.
It's Christmastime, and God is near!

THROUGH MY WINDOW

Pamela Kennedy

Art by Meredith Johnson

THE CHRISTMAS WREATH

The first December after we moved to Hawaii it was a struggle to get into the holiday spirit, so I volunteered to help with the church Christmas decorations. On the appointed day, we met in the sanctuary, and the chairperson of the decorating committee explained the general strategy for assembling the half-dozen trees, hundred or so poinsettias, swags, candelabra, ribbons, lights, and wreaths. We set to work while recorded Christmas music played softly and laughter and conversation created a convivial chorus.

It took us almost all day to complete the work, but the final effect was well worth the effort. Sparkling lights glimmered in evergreen boughs, crimson poinsettias blazed around the altar, and the center aisle was aglow with ribbons and balls of silver and gold. Then, just as we were ready to leave,

one of the women opened a cardboard box and lifted a simple cane wreath from folds of tissue paper. Its appearance was not remarkable, but I noticed the reverence with which it was handled as the wreath was centered on the front of the main pulpit. It seemed a bit out of place among the more ornate decorations. It had no ribbons, balls, or lights. In fact, its only adornment was about a hundred small fabric rosebuds clustered along one half of the woven circle. They were the kind of small, cheap, artificial buds found in craft stores and usually used to decorate favors at bridal showers.

"What's the significance of the wreath?" I asked a woman standing beside me.

"Oh, it's your first Christmas here, isn't it?" she replied, smiling. "Wait until Christmas Eve. You'll find out then." I waited.

On Christmas Eve, I showed up with my family in tow. Candlelight softened the sharp edges of the cross suspended over the altar, and the evergreens and poinsettias filled the air with spicy sweetness. When the string quartet began the strains of an ancient lullaby, even the tiniest members of the congregation quieted, and the hush of expectation spread over us all.

Soon we were singing the familiar carols of Christmas—"Joy to the World" and "Hark the Herald Angels Sing"—but I was waiting for the explanation of the Christmas wreath. What could that simple circle mean in the midst of all the grandeur? The pastor spoke and the choir sang, the children read the traditional scriptures from the Gospel of Luke. The service was almost ended when a young mother walked to the front of the sanctuary, carrying a child and leading a little boy by the hand. She took her place behind a simple wooden podium, hitched the sleeping child up higher on her hip, and folded the little boy close to her side with her other arm.

"Last Christmas," she began, "we each took a Christmas rose as the bunch was passed down our pew. I almost didn't let James take one because I didn't think he understood the purpose of the rosebuds. But it was Christmas, and I didn't want to make him unhappy." She stroked the silky brown hair on the little boy's head, and he looked up at her and grinned.

"Well, I kind of forgot about the rosebud after Christmas. Work was demanding, being a parent was exhausting, and life seemed to rush along at a hectic pace. At the hospital where I'm a nurse in the neo-natal unit, we care for high-risk babies, and the stress takes its toll. Yet in the midst of all that busyness, there was a baby, a little boy, who seemed to draw my attention. He was weak and sick, and no one ever came to see him. I checked his chart and spoke with the doctor and learned that this little fellow had been born with severe illnesses. Unable to help even herself, his mother had relinquished him to the care of the state. The little boy needed a family, but because of his health problems, he was an unlikely candidate for adoption. Day after day, whenever I had a free moment, I stood beside his crib, stroking his tiny arms and legs with my fingers, humming "Jesus Loves Me," willing him to get better. By March, little Jonathan, as we had named him, was strong enough to leave the hospital and go to a foster home. But I couldn't get him out of my mind—or my heart. And so, after much prayer, I applied to adopt him. We brought Jonathan home last summer; and the evening of his first day with us, James brought me a tiny red rosebud and asked if I would send it back to Pastor Dan at the church. When I asked him why, he told me that Pastor had invited us each to take a rosebud on Christmas Eve and to let it remind us to pray for something that we would trust God to do, and that when our prayer was answered, to send it back with a note and he would place that rosebud on next year's Christmas wreath to remind us all that God answers prayers. Then James handed me his rosebud and said simply, 'I prayed for a brother.'"

The young woman patted the chubby cheek of the child sleeping in her arms and said softly, "This is Jonathan, the answer to James's rosebud prayer."

As the young mother returned to her seat, little girls dressed in their Christmas finery walked down the aisles, handing small bouquets of red rosebuds to the individuals seated at the end of each pew. The organ played "Silent Night," and the bouquets were passed down the rows as each person removed a flower. As the service ended, the pastor reminded us of the hope shared that first Christmas and encouraged us each to have faith in the power of God to do great and wonderful things in response to our prayers. "It might take a week, a few months, or even years," he said, "but God is faithful, and we must be too."

I left the service and tucked the rosebud into my purse. I knew just what I would pray about. And when my prayer was answered, I too would send my flower back to take its place upon the Christmas wreath in silent testimony to the power of God to hear and answer the prayers of His people.

Pamela Kennedy is a freelance writer of short stories, articles, essays, and children's books. Wife of a retired naval officer and mother of three children, she has made her home on both U.S. coasts and currently resides in Honolulu, Hawaii.

THE BEST TO YOU FOR CHRISTMAS

Ann D. Lutz

Bright the shining Christmas star,
Bright the beams it sheds afar.
Brighter far the Babe that's born
Early on this Christmas morn.

Pure the virgin's humble heart,
Pure the care that's Joseph's part.
Purer far the Babe she bore,
Christ the Lord whom we adore.

Great the tidings angels bear,
Great the joy the shepherds share.
Greater far God's grace come down,
Born this day in David's town.

Sweet the song the angels sang,
Sweet the echoes as they rang.
Sweeter far the Child that lay
Cradled in the manger's hay.

Strong the faith the wise men hold,
Strong the desert wind blows cold.
Stronger far the King they seek:
Baby Jesus, mild and meek.

Rich the gifts the wise men bring
As they seek the newborn King.
Richer far the gifts He brings,
Jesus Christ, the King of kings.

Christ be with you Christmas night,
Rich and sweet and pure and bright.
Christ go with you through the year,
Keep you strong and hold you near.

A tiny girl is lost in the wonders of the season in THE ANGEL'S PROMISE *by artist Kathryn Andrews Fincher. Image copyright © Arts Uniq, Inc. Cookeville, Tennessee.*

TODAY IN BETHLEHEM HEAR I

John of Damascus

Today in Bethlehem hear I
Sweet angel voices singing.
All glory be to God on high,
Who peace on earth is bringing.

The virgin Mary holdeth more
Than highest heaven most holy.
Light shines on what was dark before
And lifteth up the lowly.

God wills that peace shall be on earth,
And holy exultation:
Sweet Babe, I greet Thy spotless birth
And wondrous incarnation.

Today in Bethlehem hear I
Even the lowly singing:
With angel-words they pierce the sky;
All earth with joy is ringing.

CHRISTMAS SONG

Bliss Carman

Above the weary waiting world,
Asleep in chill despair,
There breaks a sound of joyous bells
Upon the frosted air.
And o'er the humblest rooftree, lo,
A star is dancing on the snow.
What makes the yellow star to dance
Upon the brink of night?
What makes the breaking dawn to glow
So magically bright
And all the earth to be renewed
With infinite beatitude?
The singing bells, the throbbing star,
The sunbeams on the snow,
And the awakening heart that leaps
New ecstasy to know.
They all are dancing in the morn
Because a little Child is born.

*The sun bursts through the filigreed branches in
Peacham, Vermont. Photo by William H. Johnson.*

THE ANNUNCIATION

For unto us a child is born, unto us a son is given: and the government shall be upon his shoulder: and his name shall be called Wonderful, Counsellor, The mighty God, The everlasting Father, The Prince of Peace.

—Isaiah 9:6

And in the sixth month the angel Gabriel was sent from God unto a city of Galilee, named Nazareth, To a virgin espoused to a man whose name was Joseph, of the house of David; and the virgin's name was Mary. And the angel came in unto her, and said, Hail, thou that art highly favoured, the Lord is with thee: blessed art thou among women.

And when she saw him, she was troubled at his saying, and cast in her mind what manner of salutation this should be. And the angel said unto her, Fear not, Mary: for thou hast found favour with God. And, behold, thou shalt conceive in thy womb, and bring forth a son, and shalt call his name JESUS. He shall be great, and shall be called the Son of the Highest: and the Lord God shall give unto him the throne of his father David: And he shall reign over the house of Jacob for ever; and of his kingdom there shall be no end.

Then said Mary unto the angel, How shall this be, seeing I know not a man? And the angel answered and said unto her, The Holy Ghost shall come upon thee, and the power of the Highest shall overshadow thee: therefore also that holy thing which shall be born of thee shall be called the Son of God.

And Mary said, Behold the handmaid of the Lord; be it unto me according to thy word. And the angel departed from her.

—Luke 1:26–35, 38

ANNUNCIATION *by artist Bartolomeo Esteban Murillo (1617–1682).*
Image from Hermitage Museum, St. Petersburg, Russia/Superstock.

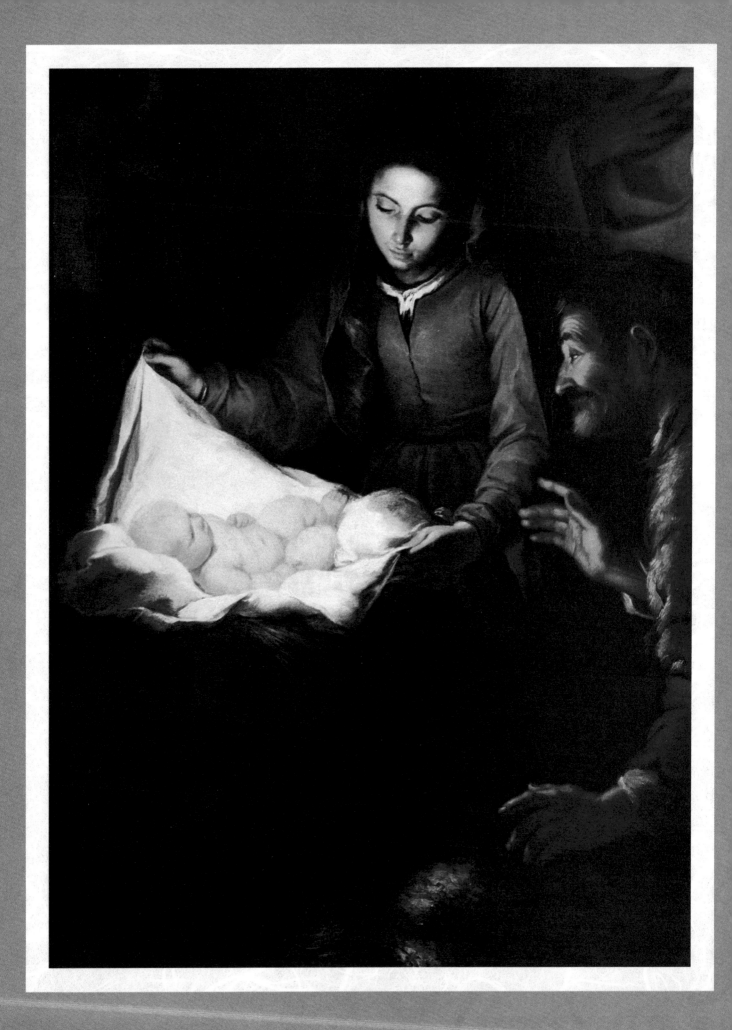

THE BIRTH OF CHRIST

*And there shall come forth a rod out of the stem of Jesse,
and a Branch shall grow out of his roots: And the spirit
of the LORD shall rest upon him, the spirit of wisdom and
understanding, the spirit of counsel and might, the spirit
of knowledge and of the fear of the LORD.*

—Isaiah 11:1, 2

And it came to pass in those days, that there went out a decree from Caesar Augustus, that all the world should be taxed. (And this taxing was first made when Cyrenius was governor of Syria.) And all went to be taxed, every one into his own city.

And Joseph also went up from Galilee, out of the city of Nazareth, into Judaea, unto the city of David, which is called Bethlehem; (because he was of the house and lineage of David:) To be taxed with Mary his espoused wife, being great with child.

And so it was, that, while they were there, the days were accomplished that she should be delivered. And she brought forth her firstborn son, and wrapped him in swaddling clothes, and laid him in a manger; because there was no room for them in the inn.

—Luke 2:1–7

ADORATION OF THE SHEPHERDS (DETAIL) *by Esteban Murillo (1617–1682). Image from Hermitage Museum, St. Petersburg, Russia/Scala/Art Resource, New York.*

THE ADORATION

But thou, Bethlehem Ephratah, though thou be little among the thousands of Judah, yet out of thee shall he come forth unto me that is to be ruler in Israel; whose goings forth have been from of old, from everlasting.

—Micah 5:2

And there were in the same country shepherds abiding in the field, keeping watch over their flock by night. And, lo, the angel of the Lord came upon them, and the glory of the Lord shone round about them: and they were sore afraid.

And the angel said unto them, Fear not: for, behold, I bring you good tidings of great joy, which shall be to all people. For unto you is born this day in the city of David a Saviour, which is Christ the Lord. And this shall be a sign unto you; Ye shall find the babe wrapped in swaddling clothes, lying in a manger.

And it came to pass, as the angels were gone away from them into heaven, the shepherds said one to another, Let us now go even unto Bethlehem, and see this thing which is come to pass, which the Lord hath made known unto us. And they came with haste, and found Mary, and Joseph, and the babe lying in a manger.

—Luke 2:8–12, 15, 16

Now when Jesus was born in Bethlehem of Judaea in the days of Herod the king, behold, there came wise men from the east to Jerusalem, Saying, Where is he that is born King of the Jews? for we have seen his star in the east, and are come to worship him.

Then Herod, when he had privily called the wise men, inquired of them diligently what time the star appeared. And he sent them to Bethlehem, and said, Go and search diligently for the young child; and when ye have found him, bring me word again, that I may come and worship him also.

When they had heard the king, they departed; and, lo, the star, which they saw in the east, went before them, till it came and stood over where the young child was.

And when they were come into the house, they saw the young child with Mary his mother, and fell down, and worshipped him: and when they had opened their treasures, they presented unto him gifts; gold, and frankincense, and myrrh.

—Matthew 2:1, 2, 7–9, 11

THE FLIGHT INTO EGYPT

The wolf also shall dwell with the lamb,
. . . and a little child shall lead them.

—Isaiah 11:6

And when they were departed, behold, the angel of the Lord appeareth to Joseph in a dream, saying, Arise, and take the young child and his mother, and flee into Egypt, and be thou there until I bring thee word: for Herod will seek the young child to destroy him.

When he arose, he took the young child and his mother by night, and departed into Egypt: And was there until the death of Herod: that it might be fulfilled which was spoken of the Lord by the prophet, saying, Out of Egypt have I called my son.

—Matthew 2:13–15

INCARNATE LOVE

Christina Rossetti

Love came down at Christmas,
    Love all lovely,
    Love divine;
Love was born at Christmas,
Star and angels gave the sign.

Worship we the Godhead,
    Love incarnate,
    Love divine;
Worship we our Jesus:
But wherewith for sacred sign?

Love shall be our token,
    Love be yours and
    Love be mine,
Love to God and all men,
Love for plea and gift and sign.

A CHRISTMAS GIFT

Clarence Hawkes

A Christmas gift Love sends to thee,
'Tis not a gift that you may see,
Like frankincense or shining gold;
Yet 'tis a gift that you may hold.

If you are lacking bread and meat,
'Twill give you heavenly bread to eat;
If you are down-trod, e'en as Job,
'Twill dress you in a seamless robe.

The gift of love in Mary's eyes,
Looked down on Jesus with surprise,
That One so great should be so small,
To point the way for kings and all.

One heart of love can move the race;
One grain of truth can change earth's face:
A Bethlehem Babe, a shepherd's rod
Have lifted mankind up to God.

A stunning Nativity is captured by artist Marianne Stokes in ANGELS AND HOLY CHILD. *Image from Fine Art Photographic Library Limited/Private Collection.*

Devotions FROM THE Heart

Pamela Kennedy

Now when Jesus was born in Bethlehem of Judaea in the days of Herod the king, behold, there came wise men from the east to Jerusalem, saying, "Where is he that is born King of the Jews? For we have seen his star in the east and are come to worship him." Matthew 2:1–2

LOOKING FOR GOD IN ALL THE WRONG PLACES

We can hardly blame the Magi for expecting to find Jesus at Herod's palace. After all, they had consulted their books and star charts and knew they were looking for a king. Where else would one go but to the royal palace in the capital city? But when they got there, no one knew anything about a new king. After a few days of consultations and research into musty old manuscripts, some priests found a reference to a town called Bethlehem. So the wise men packed up their camels and headed off. And sure enough, there, in the little town of Bethlehem, in a nondescript house, they found the baby they were seeking.

Father, this Christmas season help me to seek You in the everyday places of my life and to share Your love with abandon. Amen.

What an incredible story! If most of us were in charge of sending the Son of God to visit Earth, we'd make sure no one missed His arrival. We'd find the most popular, public place and focus the world's attention on it. But have you ever noticed how God rarely does things the way we would?

Over and over again in the Bible, God points out how His ways are not our ways. He talks about sparrows and grains of sand and single hairs and a widow's mite. In the little, out-of-the-way places of our lives, God is present. But sometimes we are so busy looking for Him in the spectacular, big, and perfect places that we miss finding Him. Like the wise men, we decide where and how God should show up; and then we go there and wait, disappointed when we don't see Him. What if we instead just went about our daily business and allowed ourselves to be surprised when God appeared in the unexpected places of life?

On that first Christmas, that's what the shepherds were doing. They were tending their sheep, and God surprised them with the good news that He had arrived in their own hometown! It has been that way through the ages all over the world. In the thirteenth century, when Francis of Assisi relinquished his inheritance to serve the poor, he wasn't looking for God, but he found Him. In the nineteenth century, when Father Damien exiled himself to live among the lepers, he wasn't looking for God, but he found Him. In the twentieth century, when Mother Teresa walked into Calcutta and embraced the dying, she wasn't looking for God, but she found Him. Today, when volunteers from all walks of life reach out to help the poor, the imprisoned, the hungry and lonely, they aren't looking for God, but they find Him.

We find God in ordinary, out of the way, messy, and unlikely places because that's where He lives. And whenever we give a cup of cold water or love the unlovely, we find Him.

That first Christmas, God didn't come to a palace, but a stable. His attendants weren't noblemen, but simple animals. His bed wasn't a golden cradle, canopied with silk; it was a simple feeding trough. This Christmas, let's not seek God in cathedrals or million-watt light displays; but instead, let's look for Him in our daily routines and in the faces of the ordinary people all around us. We will be much more likely to find Him, because when we look for Him there, we'll be looking in all the right places.

A decorated church shines in the twilight in Flint, Michigan. Photo by H. G. Ross/H. Armstrong Roberts.

The Angel and the Shepherds

A Flemish carol translated by Alfred R. Bellinger

Angel

Come, shepherds, come! Your silent sheep
No longer need your keeping.
The newborn King has come to earth,
And would you still be sleeping?
Then sing for joy and with your pipes
Set all the echoes ringing,
As oft the meadows you have filled
With dancing and with singing.

Shepherds

What voice is this at such an hour
That startles me and wakes me?
It still is night and time to sleep
Till morning overtakes me.
'Tis long before the cock will crow
And eastern sky grow yellow;
Then let me have the night in peace,
An honest, weary fellow!

Angel

Too long you rest, ye shepherd folk!
Your weariness betrays you.
For see, there dawns unearthly light
To rouse you and amaze you.
I come from heav'n to bring the news
That gladdens all creation:
A God is born in human form
Who shall be your salvation.

Shepherds

What wonder makes the darkened sky
Take on this sudden lightness?
The shades of night are swept away
By sudden magic brightness!
Indeed the Saviour it must be
In glory come to save us
And drive away the dark and fear
That did for long enslave us.

Angel

O shepherds hasten! 'Tis the time
To greet Him with thanksgiving!
To welcome Him with prayer and praise
And joy of all things living.
Arouse you comrades and repair,
Set free from death and danger
To give your hearts to God Himself
Who lies within a manger.

Shepherds

Come, comrades, come! The shepherds all
Shall run with joy beside us,
To where the Saviour waits for us;
The angel voice shall guide us.
He is our life, and all the earth
Must bend the knee before Him.
With angel hosts to lead us on,
We hasten to adore Him.

A shepherd begins the journey home in THE WINTER SHEPHERD *by artist Daniel Sherrin. Image from Fine Art Photographic Library Ltd. and by courtesy of Stern Gallery.*

The Innkeeper's Daughter

Nancy E. Berk

Oh, Mother; I have been to see the Child!
He is so precious, innocent, and fair;
The warmth of sleep has curled the baby hair
Around His little face, untried and mild.
And Mary let me hold His little hand
And fold the swaddling cloth around His feet.
To sit beside them is to know a beat
Within your heart you cannot understand.

Oh, Mother; there is music all around
That no one hears. And you can only feel
The love, and grace, and mystery abound;
That of all things, this Child, alone, is real.

And though I only went across the way,
I traveled miles—and years—with Him today.

Mary on Earth

Geraldine Ross

I wish that I had lived then, just to share
A bit of cake with her, or loiter where
She shopped for grapes or figs, or by a well
So that, while we drew water, she could tell
How sunshine lit the Christ Child's little head
And how He loved wild honey on His bread,
How Joseph whittled Him a tiny boat,
And how she had to lengthen His blue coat.
I might have seen the glory in her eyes
As she would watch Him, holding butterflies.
She must have been so friendly here, so sweet.
I wish I could have lived upon her street!

A carved Nativity captures the wonder of the first Christmas.
Photo by Paul Mayall/Gnass Photo Images.

THE YEAR THE PRESENTS DIDN'T COME

Ben Logan

Catalogs, it must be understood, were our department stores. Visitors from a marvelous place somewhere outside our world, they said Christmas was coming, that once a year a spirit of extravagance brought us a select few of all the wonderful things on display.

The catalog orders would go into the mail and our choices began to grow, becoming our own creations. Every morning when I first woke up, I would stay under the covers a moment, shut my eyes tight and try to see what was happening. After five days I decided the letter had arrived in Chicago. Two more days—no, make it three because they were busy—to find our things and ship them. Then another five days for the packages to come. I added one more day because that made it Saturday and I could run to meet the mailman myself. Mr. Holliday was driving a sled by then because there was too much snow for his Model T. He poked through the packages in the sled box. "Sorry," he said. "Not here yet."

The days crept by. Each afternoon we waited in the cold for Mr. Holliday. He would search through the sled for the packages he already knew were not there and say, "Maybe tomorrow."

On the day before Christmas we raced to the mailbox with a pail of steaming coffee for Mr. Holliday. "You know," he said, not looking at us, "I guess nothing came, but I'll just look one more time." He sorted through the packages. We knew there wasn't anything there for us. He was just trying to make us feel better, or maybe make himself feel better.

We stayed there at the mailbox looking at each other. We didn't believe it. . . . I was crying when we went to the house. Mother held me. "We'll still have Christmas, you know."

"Without our presents?"

Something changed in her face. "There's more to Christmas than presents."

When we carried the tree in and set it up in the dining room, the fresh snow began to melt into hundreds of shiny beads of water.

"Look!" Mother said. "It's already decorated."

We popped corn and made strings, the white corn alternating with the cranberries. We got out all the old ornaments, handing to Father the star that went at the very top and the others that went up high, beyond our reach. The folded paper ornaments were opened to become bright-colored balls, stars, and bells. Mother began to hum a Christmas carol. It was just like all the other remembered afternoons leading up to Christmas Eve.

The house was very still when I woke on Christmas morning. Treelike patterns of frost covered the lower half of my window, turned red-gold by the beginning color on the eastern horizon. Far out across a white meadow I could see smoke rising from the chimney of a neighbor's house, reminding me that other people were having Christmas.

For each of us there was a basket filled with English walnuts, pecans, almonds, ribbon candy, peanut brittle, chocolate stars, and one bright navel orange and a big Red Delicious apple. I sorted through my basket, silenced by the strangeness of having no presents to open and the thought of an empty day stretching ahead.

Mother went to the kitchen to work on Christmas dinner. We four boys followed and worked with her. I don't think that had ever happened before. My new toys had always captured me on Christmas morning, pulling me away into a play world that did not include anyone else.

We made sugar cookies, eating them hot and buttery right from the oven almost as fast as we cut out new ones. The chickens were already cooking, filling the house with a rich roasting smell. Junior brought his guitar into the kitchen and we sang as we worked.

Two youngsters dream of Christmas morning. Image from H. Armstrong Roberts.

Not Christmas carols. They were for later. Everyone kept talking about earlier Christmases, every other sentence beginning with "Remember the time. . . ."

Everyone was busy every minute. There were hickory nuts to crack, bowls to lick, coffee to grind, cream to whip. We kept splitting more firewood and feeding the kitchen range to keep the fire just right.

Finally, we all helped carry the steaming dishes to the dining room table with its white tablecloth that was trimmed with lace. There was a solemn moment and then the food itself, delicious and unending.

After dinner, Father left the table and put on his heavy jacket. We knew what he was going to do. Every year he took down a sheaf of oats that had been hanging on the wall since harvest and carried it outside for the birds. This time we put on our coats and went with him.

"It was something we did in Norway," he told us. "But there it would be always wheat."

He hung the oats on the big maple tree and we stepped back and waited, standing very still. A blue jay swooped in and peered at the grain. A bright red cardinal came and began to eat. Then a whole flock of English sparrows arrived, noisy and quarrelsome, reminding me of the four of us.

We cleared the snow away, brought kindling and sticks of oak from the woodshed and soon had a roaring bonfire in the yard. I ran to tell Mother, and she put on her coat and joined us.

Even then I don't think I realized how different the day had been. That is the way of Christmas stories. Their meanings have to grow with the seasons and the telling, and we only remember what we have learned by keeping the past alive.

The Sounds of Christmas

Betty H. Brown

Hear the crackle of the logs, so warmly burning,
As on this day our loved ones gather round.
This is the time when all our thoughts are turning
Toward every little Merry Christmas sound.

There is the quiet voice of snow, so gently falling,
The distant ringing of the steeple bell;
It sounds as if it is somehow calling
Us to the church which we all love so well.

Then we hear the choir, so softly singing
Their praises to the Lord in heaven above.
It seems today as if the world is ringing
With many Christmas sounds of warmth and love.

Then let the holly red be hung,
And all the sweetest carols sung,
While we with joy remember them—
The journeyers to Bethlehem.

—Frank Dempster Sherman

Childhood friends gather in song in THE CHOIR by artist Paul Barthel. Image from Christie's Images.

Christmas Past

C. David Hay
Rosedale, Indiana

The memories most endearing,
No matter where we roam,
Are those of Christmas past
In a place we knew as home.

The magic of the season
With scent of wax and pine,
The aroma from the kitchen
That beckoned us to dine.

The dancing lights upon the tree
That cast their Yuletide spell,
The joyous song of carolers,
Peace on earth, Noel.

The treasured scenes of yesteryear,
Could prayer but make them last.
Traditions of the heart live on
In dreams of Christmas past.

Christmas Colors

Ericka Northrop
Tucson, Arizona

Holly branch
And holly berry,
Red and green
And Christmas merry.
Silver stars
And lacy snow

Sparkling every place
We go.
Golden garlands,
Angel hair,
Christmas colors
Everywhere!

This Christmas Night

Raymond Bottom
Monroe, Michigan

From every window comes the flow
Of warm, inviting light,
A cheery greeting of warm love
On this Christmas night.

From snowy streets the joyful sounds
Of happy carolers singing
Harmonize with golden tones
Of church bells gladly ringing.

Every smiling, radiant face
Seems full of inner light
With the blazing fire of love
On this Christmas night.

I Sing!

Ruth K. Stroh
Cockeysville, Maryland

I sing of things I love and know:
Christmas caroling in the snow,
Lights upon the trees so bright,
Shining down on holy night.

I sing of all the girls and boys
Having joy with Christmas toys.
I sing of scented firewood;
I sing of cookies, oh, so good.

I sing of candlelights aglow;
I sing of winter winds that blow.
But best of all I like to sing
About the newborn baby King!

Season of Praise, Season of Joy

Deborah Boone
Calgary, Alberta, Canada

Christmas is the season of praise:
Hymns from a choir, praising His name,
Words lisped by children in a Nativity play,
Midnight words in a candlelit church.

Christmas is the season of joy:
Light and peace in the candle's soft glow,
Fragrance and hope from the bright evergreen,
Salvation in the smile of a baby Boy.

Editor's Note: Readers are invited to submit original poetry for possible publication in future issues of Ideals. Please send typed copies only; manuscripts will not be returned. Writers receive $10 for each published submission. Send material to Readers' Reflections, Ideals Publications, 535 Metroplex Drive, Suite 250, Nashville, Tennessee 37211.

A SLICE OF LIFE

Edgar A. Guest

Art by Eve DeGrie

WHAT DO I WANT?

What do I want for Christmas Day?
A few glad hearts about me,
Some smiles to light me on my way
As proof that you don't doubt me.
And then, if you choose,
    you may climb my knee
And smother my cheek with kisses,
And I am sure that the heart of me
Won't ache for a thing it misses.

Just tiptoe to where I sit and doze,
And give me your fond embraces,
And all of my different cares and woes
Will vanish to other places.
Just give me your love in the old-time way,
Bestow on me your caresses,
And my battered old heart on Christmas Day
Will forget all the past distresses.

Edgar A. Guest began his illustrious career in 1895 at the age of fourteen, when his work first appeared in the Detroit Free Press. His column was syndicated in more than three hundred newspapers, and he became known as "The Poet of the People."

Christmas Thoughts

Thomas John Carlisle

I close my eyes tonight and let
My thoughts roam through the days of yore
To Christmases I can't forget,
Although they come to me no more.
The fragrant smell of balsam trees,
The branches glittering with light,
The precious Christmas melodies
That I have sung again tonight,
The candles softly flickering
Down to the tallow's very stem.
And then I hear the angels sing
Above the hills of Bethlehem.

Christmas Memories

Carmen Nelson Richards

Like brilliant stars the Christmas days of childhood
Scintillate along my path of years;
And each recurring season gleams the brighter
With joyous memories my heart reveres.

Once more I see the loved ones meet together
Around the tree adorned with gifts and light
While gentle words and laughter intermingle
With anthems fragrant with this holy night.

Again I am a little child and listen
To hear my father's cherished voice in prayer,
And, like the wise men, worship at the manger
And mingle with the shepherds kneeling there.

How Many Christmases?

Doris Chalma Brock

How many Christmases
Held in your heart?
How many scenes
To remember?
Starlight and snow
And the magical glow
That you only can know
In December.

How many Christmases
Held in your heart?
How many more
To be measured?
Joy in the air,
Happy greetings to share,
These are memories rare
To be treasured.

A toy-covered wreath celebrates the season.
Photo by Nancy Matthews.

LEGENDARY AMERICANS

Nancy Skarmeas

GEORGE EASTMAN

It took only a single photograph to launch George Eastman's career in the photography business. A hard-working twenty-three-year-old in search of a path to prosperity, Eastman was, in 1877, a banker with ambition to spare. He had heard talk among the bank's wealthy clients about money to be made in real estate, and, eager to get in on the opportunity, he found a piece of property to buy. Before finalizing the purchase, however, Eastman decided to photograph the property. Because he had never before taken a photograph, he visited a local photography shop, purchased a camera, and asked for instructions. The experience that followed made Eastman forget all about real estate. From that day forward, cameras became George Eastman's business.

Eastman's first experience with a camera left him enormously frustrated by the process of taking pictures. He was overwhelmed, in fact, by the size,

weight, and complications of the photographic equipment of the day. But Eastman was not discouraged; he was inspired. He decided that there must be a better way to take pictures, and he determined that he would be the one to discover it. George Eastman entered the field of photography not out of the love of taking pictures, but out of the certainty that he could make taking pictures easier and more accessible and in the process build himself a lucrative business.

Today, without considering the simplicity, we point our cameras, press a button, and take a picture. In 1877, a single photo involved a large, awkward box camera; a heavy, metal tripod; a fragile glass plate; and a mixture of chemicals to be prepared before each exposure. Photography was the domain of professionals with the money to buy the necessary equipment, the training to use it, and the devotion to put up with the tedious process. As Eastman discovered, everyday people in 1877 did not take photographs. But what if they could, he wondered. George Eastman became quickly convinced that bringing photography to everyday Americans was a fertile opportunity.

In the late 1800s, photographers made each photo by pouring a chemical mixture onto a glass plate to form an emulsion that was sensitive to light. This was known as wet-plate photography and required that photographers carry with them plates and chemicals and that they prepare an emulsion before each photo. Obviously, this process was cumbersome, expensive, and fraught with difficulties. Made confident, perhaps, by his lack of technical knowledge, Eastman set for himself the ambitious first goal of replacing the mixed chemicals and glass plates with a pre-mixed dry emulsion on a lightweight and flexible surface.

Through research and reading, Eastman discovered that some English photographers were already working to develop "dry plates." Keeping his day hours at the bank, Eastman devoted evenings to experimenting with methods of creating a dry plate. After many long, sleepless nights, he came upon a workable formula and managed to get his plate into the hands of a local photographer, who recommended it to a large New York City photo supply store. Impressed with the innovation, this company contracted with Eastman to make the dry plates. Eastman soon had a small factory in operation. He worked nights for a time; but eventually, against the better judgment of friends and colleagues, Eastman gave up his bank job and devoted himself full-time to manufacturing dry-plate emulsions.

Unfortunately, the dry plate, which was quickly adopted by professional photographers but just as quickly improved upon by more experienced photographic chemists, was not the big money maker Eastman hoped it would be. Still hungry for financial success, he set to work on another innovation: to replace the cumbersome glass plates with something lighter and less fragile. The first step was to create a flexible film—which he did by coating paper with dry emulsion. Next, Eastman created a roller to hold his dry emulsion paper, something that could be

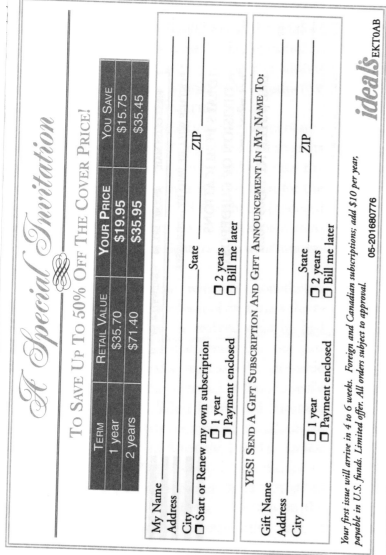

weeks, he had a new camera ready for the market.

Eastman's new Kodak camera came equipped with paper film for one hundred pictures. The owner

was then required to send the camera back to Eastman's factory, where the film was developed and the camera reloaded and returned. Although this camera began to bring photography to the people, it was still too expensive for the mass market.

Lean financial years followed, and Eastman fought off worries about the future of his company. But he kept working and in 1900 introduced the camera that finally brought him his financial breakthrough. The Brownie, as Eastman called his new piece of equipment, cost one dollar and was soon in the hands of thousands of Americans. The Brownie got Americans hooked on photography. Some went on to more sophisticated equipment; some didn't. But everyone who used this remarkable camera began to think of photographs as an indispensible way to docu... the moments of their lives. George Eastman's ...n was transforming into reality.

...Within years of the introduction of the Brownie, ...man's company was soaring financially, and ...rge Eastman became one of the wealthiest men ...merica. He had achieved, after a lifetime of work, ...ne true goal. He had built a thriving, dependable ...ness. He found himself with more money than he ...d use, and, with no wife or children, he began to ...ad that wealth. He became a noted philan...pist and a world traveler, often inviting friends to ...him on his camping trips and safaris. He retired ...h his company in 1925 at the age of seventy-five ...died seven years later.

It is at first somewhat disappointing to discover ...t the man who revolutionized photography in ...erica was not himself a photographer. To him, ...eras, film, and photographs were a business. East...n was a practical and cautious man. As a boy, he ...d seen his own mother take on boarders, cook, ...an, and scramble to support her family after her ...sband's death. He chose photography as his career ...ause he believed it offered him the prosperity to ...tect him from ever again knowing such hardship. ...t his determination and drive, his single-minded ...rsuit of excellence, and his ability to see beyond ...at was possible to what could be possible make him ...han to admire and celebrate. Anyone who has ever ...lt the evocative power of a treasured snapshot can be thankful that George Eastman chose cameras instead of real estate as the focus of his life's ambition.

HANDMADE HEIRLOOM

A grouping of family portraits captures moments, and faces, to treasure. Photo by Jerry Koser.

FAMILY PORTRAIT

Nancy Skarmeas

To my mind, there is no better family heirloom than a photograph. As precious as a beautiful family photograph is in the present, it becomes only more so with the passage of time. As memories fade, as children grow, as we all age and change and one generation replaces another, photographs keep us connected. In my own family we have so few photographs of our preceding generations that each one is a true treasure. I have vowed that my own life and the lives of my children will be better documented. I want my children to have pictures of themselves, pictures of their parents and grandparents, pictures of their cousins and friends.

But for all the endless rolls of film I have shot, I have never really attempted a true family portrait. Like most amateur photographers, I have not thought myself up to the job. My snapshots have improved greatly over the years through trial and error, and I have come up with many pictures worthy of framing. But I have never had the confidence to assemble my family together for an official portrait. I have always been hesitant to have that many people anxiously awaiting the results of my efforts. Until now, that is. My desire for a good family portrait has finally outweighed my reluctance to take on the assignment. I am planning a portrait of my parents, my brothers and sister, and the family's six grandchildren. Ambitious? Certainly. Beyond the reach of an amateur photographer? I really don't think so.

Too often I have attempted a photo haphazardly only to be disappointed by the results. So for this portrait, my watchword is preparation. I plan to combine what I have learned through my years of taking photographs with what I can glean from books on the subject and then to spend several rolls of film practicing on my own children before I attempt the big group.

What have I learned from my many years of taking photos? First, that good photographers can never take enough pictures of their subject. My main experience in this area has come through the Christmas card photos I have taken of my kids and dogs. I have come up with a few great shots and have received many compliments on my knack with a camera. What people don't know is that what they see is only one of twenty-four, thirty-six, or more shots. I have a drawer full of Christmas card rejects. There are kids crying or simply walking away, dogs blurring as they jump up to chase a squirrel, and countless shots where three or four faces are looking in three or four different directions. One that I especially like is of my son whacking one of the dogs on the head with a plastic hoe. The look of joy on his face is priceless, as is the look of tolerance on the dog's face. Not Christmas-card calibre, certainly, but memorable nonetheless. The point is, it takes a lot of exposures to get that one perfect shot.

The second lesson I have learned through trial and error is that no matter how close I first stand to my subjects, I usually need to get a few steps closer. I try to always remember to fill the frame with my subject. A related lesson: I have learned to shoot subjects on their own level. That means dogs, kids, and babies require squatting, sitting, kneeling, and even lying down. I have learned to get down on the floor and to stop worrying what I look like while doing it.

To supplement the lessons learned at the school of experience, I searched out some books on photography for amateurs. In books I found advice on posing, setting, lighting, even the best time of day and the proper way to deal with subjects ranging in age from infancy to old age. One author offered particularly good advice on group shots. Shoot down from a ladder, he said. In addition, he urged portrait takers to focus on people's faces. This advice made me think of a family portrait I once saw at a friend's house. All the members of her family are extremely tall, and the photographer had taken the shot at an upward angle. He or she had not thought to zoom in on the faces, so what you see in the photo is a looming line of long legs and big feet with tiny-looking heads in the distance.

One piece of advice I saw repeated several times was to turn off the flash. This advice I found both frightening and inspirational. I know from experience that flash more often than not ruins photos. Whether it is the red-eye glare or the washed-out skin tones, I am rarely happy with photos taken indoors. So, I decided to put aside my fears, turn off my flash, and shoot my family portrait with only natural light. Intrepid amateur photographers who wish to do the same should seek out books on photography and learn about how to use natural lighting.

Of course, we would-be portrait photographers should not get so caught up in the quest for the perfect portrait that we forget that almost every photo of our families is worth keeping. From one of my practice sessions with my children, I must have ten shots of my baby girl sitting in front of her five-year-old brother as he makes his trademark goofy face. That is what five-year-old boys do in front of cameras, and although I might not need ten angles on that face, I do want to remember it. And there is one beautiful, sunlit shot of a baby looking adoringly at her happy brother, who was caught laughing by the camera before he thought to make his silly face. The kids aren't perfectly centered in the picture, and it may never sit framed on my mantel, but it will always make me smile.

So, am I ready to take the family portrait? This is what I know so far. A good family portrait can be taken by an amateur, but not by someone unwilling to take a lot of pictures and make a lot of mistakes. It means being prepared and thinking about every detail: who will be in the picture, what they will wear, where they will pose, how they will pose. It means deciding in advance what time of day, what source of lighting, what angle, and the list goes on. If there are children, as I have learned, make sure they are happy and rested. Take a whole roll and take it quickly, but not so fast that you neglect to properly frame the subject. Read books and learn, and don't forget to have a sense of fun and adventure.

The quest for the perfect family portrait is an enticing challenge for someone who loves photography and loves chronicling the life of her family. A professional could take a beautiful portrait of my family. The lighting would be perfect, the posing organized, the background carefully chosen. But he or she wouldn't know how we relate to each other, what to say to make us all laugh, what we want to remember about each other. These things I surely know. And that knowledge, combined with a lot of practice and patience, might just make for a spectacular portrait.

Christmas Photo

Joan Stephen

Every year at Christmas
We sat beneath the tree
While Father took our picture,
Holding presents on our knee.

We still were in our nighties,
Old slippers on our feet.
The hot oatmeal was ready,
But we took no time to eat.

No one had to tell us
To laugh or grin or smile;
Surrounded by the brand new toys
We did it all the while.

Our expressions were delightful,
And life was full of fun,
Especially at Christmas
When all of us were young.

Today we hold the photos;
Laugh or cry at what we see,
Each with some remembrance
Of those times beneath the tree.

Christmas Portrait

Dan A. Hoover

Fireplace flickering in the twilight,
Christmas treetop, ceiling tall,
Chains from bright wallpaper samples,
Red leaves saved from frosty fall,
Strings of Grandma's snowy popcorn,
Tinsel silvering each bough,
Stockings hanging at the mantel;
Memory paints them clearly now.

Children are sure to find delights beneath this festive tree.
Photo by Daniel Dempster.

Old-Fashioned Christmas

Edna Jaques

I like old-fashioned things at Christmastime—
Old-fashioned lights and tinsel on a tree,
Red candles lighted in a quiet room,
A grandma with a baby on her knee;

The smell of cedar in the living room,
Pinecones with bits of silver on their tips,
A holly wreath tied with a scarlet bow,
The smell of wax when a tall candle drips,

The taste of mincemeat from a covered crock,
Brown Christmas cake, mulled cider in a jug,
Gay parcels piled behind the Christmas tree,
Warm firelight playing on a crimson rug;

The brown skin of the turkey rich and good,
Old-fashioned dressing made with sage and bread,
Rich gravy spilling from a golden bowl,
Cranberry jelly glowing bright and red,

The mother with a clean print apron on,
Dishing the dinner up with happy pride;
Dad carving turkey, heaping up the plates,
Laying the wishbone snugly to one side.

I love old-fashioned things on Christmas Day,
Snow on the ground, a church across the way.

At Christmastime, these are the things I know:
Fragrance of pine, air frosted, keen with snow;
Laughter of children, raised in glad surprise;
Breathless expectancy; the smiling eyes
Of friends with gifts white-clad and ribbon-tied;
Odor of good things cooking. There abide
The dearest things I know in all the earth:
Home and the loved ones, friendship, song, and mirth.

—Author Unknown

Ideals'
Family Recipes

To many families, baking Christmas cookies is as much a part of the holidays as trimming the tree. Try these scrumptious cookie recipes, some traditional and some with a twist, on your next baking day. Send a typed copy to Ideals Publications, 535 Metroplex Drive, Suite 250, Nashville, TN 37211. *We pay $10 for each recipe published.*

Orange-Carrot Cookies
Doris Tinker of Shell Knob, Missouri

2 cups all-purpose flour
2 teaspoons baking powder
¼ teaspoon salt
1 cup butter
¾ cup granulated sugar
1 cup mashed, cooked carrots

1 egg, beaten
1 teaspoon almond extract
2 cups powdered sugar
1 tablespoon melted butter
Zest and juice of 1 orange

Preheat oven to 350° F. In a large bowl, sift together flour, baking powder, and salt. Set aside. In a large bowl, cream butter with sugar. Add carrots, egg, and extract; mix well. Gradually stir in dry ingredients. Mix well. Drop by teaspoonsful onto a greased baking sheet. Bake 12 to 15 minutes or until set. Remove to a wire rack to cool. In a small bowl, combine powdered sugar, melted butter, and orange zest. Stir in a small amount of orange juice until sugar is dissolved. Continue adding juice until glaze reaches desired consistency. Brush glaze over cookies while still warm. Makes 2 to 3 dozen cookies.

Fruitcake Cookies
Janice E. Leffew of Seattle, Washington

2 cups all-purpose flour
½ teaspoon baking soda
½ teaspoon salt
1 teaspoon ground allspice
1 cup brown sugar, packed

½ cup vegetable oil
¼ cup water
1 egg, beaten
1 cup glacéed fruit
1 cup chopped pecans

Preheat oven to 400° F. In a large bowl, sift together flour, baking soda, salt, and allspice. Set aside. In a large bowl, combine brown sugar, oil, water, and egg. Mix well. Gradually stir in dry ingredients. Mix well. Stir in fruit and pecans. Drop dough by rounded teaspoonsful 2 inches apart onto an ungreased baking sheet. Bake 8 to 10 minutes or until golden. Immediately remove to wire rack to cool. Makes 3 dozen.

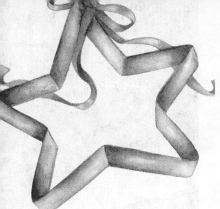

Nutmeg Cookies
Lorene Beeler of Fresno, California

2 cups all-purpose flour
1 teaspoon nutmeg
1 teaspoon baking powder
⅛ teaspoon baking soda
½ teaspoon salt

1 egg, beaten
½ cup butter, softened
¾ cup granulated sugar
4 tablespoons plus ⅓ cup
   milk, divided

½ cup shortening
1 16-ounce box powdered sugar
1 teaspoon vanilla

In a large bowl, sift together flour, nutmeg, baking powder, baking soda, and salt. Set aside. In a large bowl, beat egg with butter. Add sugar and 4 tablespoons milk and beat until well blended. Gradually stir in dry ingredients. Chill dough 30 minutes or until firm.

Preheat oven to 375° F. Roll dough out on floured surface until approximately ⅛-inch thick. Use cookie cutters to cut out shapes. Place on greased baking sheet. Bake 10 to 12 minutes or until golden. Remove to wire rack to cool. In a small bowl, make icing by creaming shortening. Add powdered sugar and ⅓ cup milk, alternating until well blended. Stir in vanilla. Brush icing over cooled cookies. Makes approximately 2 dozen cookies.

Triple Surprise Cookies
Dorothy Rieke of Julian, Nebraska

½ cup plus 3 tablespoons
   butter, divided
½ cup brown sugar, packed
1 egg yolk
½ teaspoon almond extract

¼ teaspoon salt
1½ cups all-purpose flour
Walnut halves
12 large marshmallows
1 cup semi-sweet chocolate chips

In a large bowl, cream ½ cup butter with sugar. Stir in egg yolk, extract, and salt. Gradually add flour. Mix well. Place dough onto waxed paper and form into a roll. Wrap in waxed paper and chill until firm.

Preheat oven to 350° F. Slice dough into ¼-inch-thick slices. Press a walnut half into the underside of each cookie and place on an ungreased baking sheet. Bake 10 minutes or until set. Remove baking sheet from oven; place ½ of a large marshmallow on the top of each hot cookie. Return to oven until marshmallows are melted. Remove from oven and cool slightly. In the top of a double boiler, combine chocolate chips and 3 tablespoons butter. Stir until melted. Spoon one teaspoon of chocolate mixture over top of each cookie. Remove to wire rack. Makes approximately 2 dozen cookies.

Heritage

Laura Emerson Gradick

This table, beautiful and fine and strong,
Was built at Grandpa's order, long ago
When perfect craftsmanship was all the rule.
I loved the table as a child, the glow
Of polished wood, the curve of pedestal;
At Christmastime its great length stirred my pride,
Grandma and Grandpa at the head and foot,
Aunts, uncles, cousins filling either side.

They all are gone, but I can still recall
The merry, laughing faces, joyous times,
The tantalizing odors of the feasts,
The clink of silver heard through Christmas chimes.
The table, with its memories, now is mine.
Next Christmas I shall sit in Grandma's place
With loving thoughts of those who owned it first,
And ask their great-great-grandson to say grace.

*Once again we are weaving
the tapestry that is Christmas.*

—Polly McKinstry

*An heirloom table beckons its family to the holiday feast.
Photo by Jessie Walker.*

From My Garden Journal

Lisa Ragan

PAPERWHITE NARCISSUS

In my extended family, Christmas has always meant special family gatherings. Often we would gather at my Aunt Shirley's beautiful Victorian home and sing Christmas carols around her baby grand piano. The smells of pumpkin pie, peppermint candy canes, and clove-studded oranges intermingle in my memory, but one unmistakable scent overpowers them all: paperwhite narcissus. Aunt Shirley always displayed pots of blooming paperwhite narcissus in her home at Christmas; and the flower's distinctive, sweet aroma will forever take me back in my mind to those heartwarming gatherings with my family.

The name *narcissus* comes to us from the stories of ancient Greece. In Greek mythology, the goddess Nemesis punished the beautiful youth Narcissus because he rebuffed the love of all fair maidens who saw him. When Narcissus bent over a pool of water for a drink, Nemesis caused him to become so enraptured with his own reflection that he could not move. Narcissus then wasted away while staring at his own beautiful face in the pool until he finally grew roots and turned into a flower.

Today, the name *narcissus* serves as the official botanical name encompassing seventy species and more than twenty-thousand daffodil cultivars in existence (daffodil is the common name). I have heard gardeners argue about whether a particular cultivar is a daffodil or a narcissus, but the truth is that they are one and the same. To confuse matters even more, my southern relatives call them jonquils, but this moniker has a historical explanation. Colonists to the New World brought with them from England *narcissus jonquilla*, which is why the name *jonquil* has become a synonym for daffodils.

Paperwhite narcissus (*narcissus tazetta*) originated in the Mediterranean region but has also been identified in numerous Asian countries for hundreds of years. The Victorian period in the United States saw a rising fascination with horticulture in general, including indoor and outdoor home gardens. The Victorians enjoyed forcing narcissus indoors, and the bulbs performed especially well in cold, drafty parlors.

Sometimes called the Christmas daffodil, paperwhites are an ideal plant for a beginner to force indoors during the winter months because as a warm-weather bulb it needs no chilling period in order to bloom. Paperwhite bulbs often come to us from the warm climate of Israel and are available at nurseries from early autumn through the Christmas season. Most bulbs have been carefully selected, so just check for any excessive softness or any signs of mold. Keep bulbs cool and dry until you're ready to plant them, but do plant within one month of purchase or they may rot and fail to flower.

Paperwhite narcissus produces plants with clusters of three to twenty flowers on each short, thick stem. Their broad, grayish-green leaves provide a lovely complement to the delicate, fragrant flowers. Tazettas are available in a number of cultivars with varying colors and aromas. Paperwhite Grandiflora is by far the most popular tazetta daffodil, but if you prefer a softer, more musky fragrance, try Israel, which is the color of creamy butter, or Bethlehem or Nazareth, both of which grow into plants with shorter and brighter flowers. Galilee and Jerusalem both offer a more delicate scent than some other varieties. For an interesting color variation, try Grand Soleil d'Or, which boasts golden yellow blossoms with orange cups.

About six weeks before you want blossoming plants (mid-November if Christmas is your deadline), pot the bulbs and place them in a well-lit, cool room no warmer than sixty degrees Fahrenheit. Some gardeners pot paperwhite bulbs every two weeks throughout the winter in order to enjoy the promise of spring throughout the coldest months. The bulbs can be grown in a multitude of media, including regular potting soil, small pebbles or gravel, marbles, or seashells. Aunt Shirley often potted her paperwhites in glass vases filled with bright red cranberries and water—a stunning color combination when the blossoms appeared at Christmas.

Not only can you choose an unusual planting medium for your forced paperwhites, but you can also choose an unusual container in which to grow them. Gardeners employ truly inventive containers for their paperwhites, including a fish bowl (minus the fish), a hollowed-out log, or a watering can. Bulb pans can also be used, or you can purchase an hour-glass-shaped vase from your florist or nursery that is designed specifically for forcing paperwhite bulbs. Fill the bottom of the vase with water and set the bulb in the top portion, with just the base of the bulb touching the water. If you choose a conventional flowerpot and potting soil, use a pot with drainage holes and keep the bulb well watered. Any of the more unique containers should have no drainage holes and should be filled with water to just the base of the bulb (watering any higher could cause the bulb to rot).

When the first blossoms begin to appear, move your paperwhites out of the direct sunlight and stake as needed. Berried twigs can provide a holiday touch and stake your paperwhites at the same time. Some gardeners choose to tie the shoots together with raffia or colorful ribbon in order to support the blossoms. Experts also recommend that you keep your paperwhites in a cool location at night in order to prolong the blooming time. The system for forcing the bulb generally weakens it so much that the spent bulbs are best relegated to the compost bin. Paperwhites can be grown outdoors in hot climates; check with your local nursery to see if you live in one of the suitable zones. For outdoor enjoyment, paperwhites should be planted in October or November in full sun and will bloom by December or January.

This Christmas I've decided to continue Aunt Shirley's tradition of growing potted paperwhite narcissus indoors to enjoy during the holidays. I can already picture my family gathering round my piano, singing the same old Christmas carols, and enjoying the smells of the season, including the most pervasive scent of all: the sweet aroma of the paperwhites wafting through my home.

Lisa Ragan tends her small but mighty city garden in Nashville, Tennessee, with the help of her two shih-tzu puppies, Clover and Curry.

COLLECTOR'S CORNER

MINIATURE CHRISTMAS VILLAGES

Laurie Hunter

Some people have a difficult time getting into the Christmas spirit. I am not one of those people. I look forward to the holidays with the onset of autumn, begin shopping by late October, decorate the day after Thanksgiving, and take a week of vacation during December to revel in the festivities.

Despite my love of the holiday hustle and bustle, my favorite part of the season is a little ritual I keep all to myself. One night after the children are in bed and my husband is busy with some project of his own, I douse the lights in the living room so that twinkling Christmas tree lights are the only illumination. Sitting cross-legged on the hardwood floor, I begin unpacking my ever-expanding collection of miniature Christmas villages, a collection of buildings and props that fascinates me more and more each year.

First, I peel back sheets of tissue paper from the humble stable—a bisque piece that I hand-painted in grade school. I had spent so much time painting the stable that no time had been left to paint any people to go with it. So for years, my stable housed little figures sculpted from clay.

Next, I unwrap tiny china figurines with perfect faces, perfect hands, perfect expressions: an awe-struck Joseph, a meek Mary, a rejoicing angel, three wise onlookers, and a tiny Baby tucked in a manger. The figures were given to me by my parents on the first Christmas I celebrated with my husband.

Looking back to that first Christmas as a newly wed couple, the traditional-looking Nativity scene did look beautiful in our otherwise undecorated apartment, but it didn't seem com-

My children turn to discover that an entire city has sprung up under our tree while they slept.

plete. Where was the little town of Bethlehem? Surely a "town" must contain more than just one building. A collectible fascination began to take root as I searched for pieces to help tell the complete Christmas story.

From heaps of tissue, I continue unearthing more recent additions to my collection. A little carpentry shop emerges from the wrappings and is placed on the outskirts of town. I picked it up at an open antique market on a shopping spree in New York City. Purchased recently at a neighborhood department store, a two-story, lighted gatekeeper's dwelling is the largest and heaviest piece in my collection. Made from ceramic, it is fashioned to reflect the architecture of Bible times.

I then lovingly open other bundles of surprises, revealing handfuls of camels, cypress trees, and sandy rocks. There is a donkey too, and a craggy mountain backdrop—everything I need to re-create the ancient scene of Christ's birth, a desert oasis in the middle of my modern-day living room.

Once the village is complete, I curl up on the sofa and bask in the quaint scene. In the morning, the children scurry in to find that I've fallen asleep on the sofa. They kiss me into awareness and ask what I'm doing sleeping out here like the family cat. I tell them I've been waiting to catch a glimpse of the elves who always set up our Christmas village, but I've missed them again. They turn to discover that an entire city has sprung up under our tree while they slept. I smile triumphantly behind their backs.

I'd say the Christmas village custom is just for the children, but I know better. I keep the tradition going because it just wouldn't feel like Christmas without it. Sometimes it seems my village is the only tiny aspect of the holiday that doesn't change. A neat row of small buildings, a tiny desert setting, a diminutive recreation of the humblest of villages—this is my own little town of Bethlehem.

O LITTLE TOWN

If you would like to collect tiny Christmas villages, the following information may be helpful.

A LITTLE HISTORY

Miniature Christmas villages originated in Germany and primarily depicted the Nativity scene. In the nineteenth century, their popularity spread to the United States, where tiny trees, churches, houses, animals, and figurines were added to the tradition. Today, there are numerous manufacturers of ceramic and porcelain villages throughout the world.

GETTING STARTED

What makes these tiny villages such a big hit? Christmas villages appeal to so many people because there are so many different varieties to collect. To get started, first clarify the type of village you want to create. Then, purchase your display's "centerpiece"—a favorite from which the entire town will be built; with careful planning and searching, an enduring collection will grow from there.

FINDING THEM

You can collect Christmas villages year-round by frequenting holiday shops, antique booths, estate sales, and flea markets. When someone asks what you want for Christmas, request additions to your collection, which, for the gift-giver, are both affordable and fun to select. Collecting villages can even become a family activity, with each person adding his or her own favorites to the mix.

WHAT TO EXPECT

Christmas villages are popular collectibles. Clubs have been formed to share display tips among collectors, and holiday expositions are held to showcase personal collections. Entire magazines cater to the Christmas village collector. This kind of demand has created a surge in pricing. Expect to pay anywhere from thirty to one hundred dollars for a new piece; second-hand pieces can be found for a bit less. "Retired"

At Christmastime, miniature village collectors might choose to re-create the little town of Bethlehem. Photo courtesy Department 56.

pieces can cost much more, depending on their market worth. (Current values are listed in a collector's green book.) One church in particular, from which the original mold was broken after a limited number had been made, is said to be worth fifteen thousand dollars!

DISPLAY TIPS

A wealth of accessories is available to help the budding village hobbyist create a realistic and beautiful Christmas village. Supplies can be found at holiday and gift shops, craft stores, and related web sites. Or simply use your imagination. Position natural twigs to resemble trees. Artfully arrange cotton fiberfill to hint at new-fallen snow. Enlist the children's miniature dolls and stuffed animals to inhabit the village. Add a mirror to serve as an enchanting lake or pond. Encircle the town with a model railroad train set. Then spotlight the vignette with candles or tiny white lights.

Picture

Craig E. Sathoff

A twilight frame of mellow hue,
A gently winding brook,
A narrow path that birches guard
With tall and stately look.

A little cottage small and warm,
An evergreen beside,
A lazy stream of curling smoke
That trails through countryside.

A picture that is beautiful
And yet a dream come true;
For waiting in our cottage door,
My dear, I can see you.

At the End of Day

Emily Buzelle

The sun has set, and the night
Is mantling another day.
I look at the hill across the pond
As I homeward make my way.

I gaze at the wooded slope
As it rises high in the west.
The green of the pines in deep silhouette
Is a blending of tones with the rest.

Ice-blue at the back of the hill,
With a star shimmering through;
A brisk west wind with a winter tang,
And my steps turn home to you.

A father and son head toward home in the painting FAIRFAX VILLAGE
COVERED BRIDGE *by artist Eric Sloane. Image from Christie's Images.*

Christmas Wish

Brian F. King

May your shining Christmas star
Bring all the Yuletide joys there are;
And may your windows be alight
With peace and love on Christmas night.
May Bethlehem its story tell
To all who in your household dwell;
And, most of all, for this I pray,
The Christ Child bless your Christmas Day.

Oh, may your table candles light
A Christmas Eve of sheer delight;
And may your heart on Christmas morn
Rejoice the Saviour has been born.
Oh, may your household rafters ring
With carols children love to sing,
And would that I were there to see
The love that lights your Christmas tree.

I pray your wealth of Christmas cheer
Be followed by a glad New Year,
And that your hearthstone keep the blaze
Of Christmas joy through winter days.
May all your loved ones come to share
The bounties of your Christmas fare.
All this and more be yours I pray
To bless your house on Christmas day.

May Your Christmas Be Blessed

Mildred L. Jarrell

May your Christmas be blessed
With the joys of old,
Filling the heart with gifts untold.
Friends at the doorway
Bustling good cheer,
Carolers singing the songs we hold dear.

May your Christmas be blessed
With the homiest things,
The warmth of a hearth, a kettle that sings,
A snug little house with loved ones near,
And a heart filled with blessings
To last through the year.

A young girl remembers the season of giving.
Photo by Superstock.

PRAYER FOR THE NEW YEAR

Robert Louis Stevenson

Lord, we thank Thee for this place
In which we dwell;
For the love that unites us;
For the peace accorded us this day;
For the hope with which we expect the morrow;
For the health, the work, the food,
And the bright skies that make our lives delightful;
For our friends in all parts of the earth.
Give us courage, gaiety, and quiet mind.
Spare to us our friends, soften to us our enemies.
Bless us, if it may be, in all our innocent endeavors.
If it may not, give us the strength
To encounter that which is to come,
That we may be brave in peril,
Constant in tribulation, temperate in wrath
And in all changes of fortune,
And, down to the gates of death,
Loyal and loving one to another. Amen.

A GREETING

Fra Giovanni

I salute you:
There is nothing I can give you
which you have not;
But there is much that,
while I cannot give you, you can take.
No heaven can come to us unless our
hearts find rest in it today. Take heaven.
No peace lies in the future which is not
hidden in the present. Take peace.
The gloom of the world is but a shadow;
behind it, yet within our reach, is joy.
Take joy.
And so, at this Christmastime, I greet you,
With the prayer that for you,
now and forever,
The day breaks and the shadows flee away.

A Montana farm in the Scapegoat Wilderness offers a peaceful scene to greet the new year. Photo by Carr Clifton.

Readers' Forum

Snapshots from Our Ideals Readers

Upper left: Joe and Flo Thomas of Auburn, Alabama, share this snapshot of their four-year-old grandson, Christopher Thomas, who is watching with delight as the snowflakes float past him. "Kiffer" (as he calls himself) is the son of George and Jane Thomas.

Upper right: Monroe and Nancy Myers of St. Louis, Missouri, share this photo of their grandson, Garrett Michael Myers, age ten months. When Garrett's mother held him up to the front door wreath to say a last goodbye to his grandparents, the couple was able to snap this adorable shot through the glass door.

Lower left: Even though the recent snowfall wasn't very deep, Brant, Kylee, and Brooke Probst managed to build an impressive snowman and snow puppy while visiting their grandmother, NaDene S. Probst, in Midway, Utah. NaDene tells us that Brant, Kylee, and Brooke are only three of her twenty-eight wonderful grandchildren.

Upper left: As a city girl, Erin Meredith Mootrey doesn't get to play in the snow very often. But a recent trip to see Grandma and Grandpa (Ginny and Erwin Eckson) in Williamstown, Vermont, offered two-year-old Erin plenty of time for making snowballs. Erin is the daughter of Lynelle and Scott Mootrey.

Upper right: Mrs. Loye P. Rowe of Hickory, North Carolina, sent us this photo of her two granddaughters, Hallie (left) and Kendall (right) Rhoads, who live in Georgia. Though their southern Christmas wasn't white, the girls donned snowflake sweaters to help put them in the spirit of the season.

Lower right: Sharon Johnson of Carrier Mills, Illinois, sends us this photo of her granddaughter, Macey Jo Donahue, dressed in a celestial outfit for the family's Christmas card portrait. Sharon says that Macey is an angel inside and out, and not only during the holidays. Macey is the daughter of Rebellie Donahue.

THANK YOU Joe and Flo Thomas, Monroe and Nancy Myers, NaDene S. Probst, Ginny and Erwin Eckson, Mrs. Loye P. Rowe, Sharon Johnson, and Irene Woodliff for sharing your family photographs with *Ideals*. We hope to hear from other readers who would like to share snapshots with the *Ideals* family. Please include a self-addressed, stamped envelope if you would like the photos returned. Keep your original photographs for safekeeping and send duplicate photos along with your name, address, and telephone number to:

Readers' Forum
Ideals Publications
535 Metroplex Drive, Suite 250
Nashville, Tennessee 37211

Above and below: Irene Woodliff of Lebanon, Tennessee, wanted to share these photographs of her grandchildren, Keaton and Noah Woodliff (ages four years and eight months). Keaton and Noah, who are the children of Tommy and Karen Woodliff, were happy to be on chimney watch last Christmas Eve.

Publisher, Patricia A. Pingry
Editor, Michelle Prater Burke
Designer, Travis Rader
Copy Editor, Amy Johnson
Editorial Assistant, Patsy Jay
Contributing Editors, Lansing Christman, Pamela Kennedy, Nancy Skarmeas, and Lisa Ragan

ACKNOWLEDGMENTS

FARRAR, JOHN. "Bundles" from *Songs for Parents.* Copyright © 1922 by John Farrar. Used by permission of Yale University Press. GUEST, EDGAR A. "What Do I Want." Used by permission of the author's estate. JAQUES, EDNA. "Old-Fashioned Christmas." Copyright © in Canada by Thomas Allen & Son Limited. LOGAN, BEN. "The Year the Presents Didn't Come" from *Christmas Remembered.* Initially published by NorthWord Press. Copyright © 1997 by Ben Logan. Used by permission of Fran Collin, Literary Agent. TABER, GLADYS. "December" from *The Stillmeadow Road.* Copyright © 1962 by Gladys Taber and renewed © 1990 by Constance Taber. Used by permission of Brandt & Brandt Literary Agents, Inc. Our sincere thanks to the following authors whom we were unable to locate: Brian F. King for "Christmas Wish"; Julia H. Strong for "Remembered Christmas" from *Postlude to Mendelssohn;* and Emily May Young for "Wondrous Love" from *Into the Light.*

Now in a magnificent collection entitled . . .
HYMNS OF PRAISE, discover the stories behind our most beloved hymns

In the message found in our favorite hymn we are encouraged, inspired, and strengthened in times of need. But have you ever wondered what inspired the hymn writers? Who encouraged them? What strengthened them?

Author Pamela Kennedy devoted many, many hours to researching the lives of the authors and composers who created these beloved hymns and discovered many inspiring stories of how these hymns came to be written. As you browse through these stories, you'll discover other heartwarming stories of faith and courage. You can enjoy playing and singing each hymn as well. The words and music to all of the hymns are included and printed on non-glare paper. All of the verses that were originally written are also included along with a simple-to-play musical arrangement.

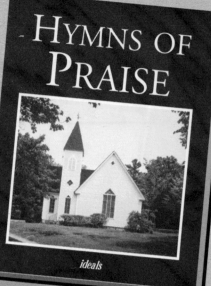

160 pages, full color throughout, heavy-weight enamel stock, deluxe hardcover binding.

If you are a person who loves these wonderful hymns . . . if you ever need encouragement in the face of life's obstacles. . . if you love music and enjoy learning more about the composers . . . then you owe it to yourself to take advantage of our offer of a free look at this collection of the stories of men and women of faith.

Return the reply card today to preview HYMNS OF PRAISE for 30-days FREE . . . and receive a FREE *Words of Praise* Booklet.

BUSINESS REPLY MAIL
FIRST-CLASS MAIL PERMIT NO. 38 CARMEL NY

POSTAGE WILL BE PAID BY ADDRESSEE

NO POSTAGE
NECESSARY
IF MAILED
IN THE
UNITED STATES

GUIDEPOSTS
PO BOX 797
CARMEL NY 10512-9905

⟨≈ FREE EXAMINATION CERTIFICATE ≈⟩

YES! I'd like to examine HYMNS OF PRAISE for 30-days FREE. If after 30 days I am not delighted with it, I may return it and owe nothing. If I decide to keep it, I will be billed $24.95, plus postage and handling. In either case, the FREE *WORDS OF PRAISE* Booklet is mine to keep.

Please print your name and address:

MY NAME

MY ADDRESS

CITY   STATE   ZIP

Total copies ordered _____

❏ Please Bill Me ❏ Charge My: ❏ MasterCard   ❏ Visa

Credit Card #:

Expiration Date: _____

Signature _____

No need to send money now. We will bill you later.

Allow 4 weeks for delivery.
Orders subject to credit approval.

15/201674280

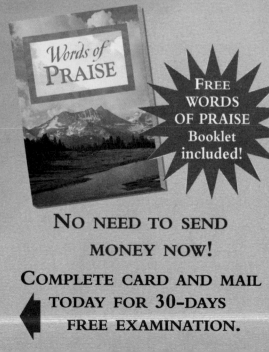

NO NEED TO SEND MONEY NOW!

COMPLETE CARD AND MAIL TODAY FOR 30-DAYS FREE EXAMINATION.

FREE WORDS OF PRAISE Booklet included!